Original title:
Life's Meaning: Not Available in Stores

Copyright © 2025 Creative Arts Management OÜ
All rights reserved.

Author: Giselle Montgomery
ISBN HARDBACK: 978-1-80566-285-3
ISBN PAPERBACK: 978-1-80566-580-9

The Alchemy of Solitude

In my room, I'm a king of the quirks,
Juggling pizzas and dirty forks.
My socks hold meetings, a cozy affair,
Debating how long I can go with this hair.

Silent Conversations with the Self

Talking to myself, what a splendid chat,
He insists he can do better than that.
I argue back with the tea in my hand,
He thinks he's a genius, I think he's quite bland.

Dreams That Defy the Checkout

In dreams, I stroll down aisles of delight,
Where candy clouds burst in glorious flight.
I find a cart filled with wishes, no bills,
But then I wake up, and my back just kills.

Crumbs of Wisdom in Forgotten Corners

In the couch, there's treasure, old chips and some lint,
Each crumb a lesson, or so I would hint.
The vacuum's my foe, it just doesn't see,
These nuggets of thought, they're so precious to me.

Mirrors that Reflect the Unseen

In stores, they sell the latest trends,
But wisdom hides where laughter bends.
You won't find joy on any shelf,
It's lurking close, within yourself.

The price tags lie, they start to sway,
With every wrinkle, they decay.
The mirror shows what's really there,
A twinkle bright, a goofy stare.

Beyond the Aisles of Material

Past the aisles of shiny things,
Where clutter packs and the chaos sings.
A little dance beneath the stars,
Reveals the wealth of laughs, not cars.

You can't buy smiles, they're free to share,
Watch them sprout from thin old air.
The nonsense is where riches thrive,
Amidst the quirks, we come alive.

The Essence of Fleeting Moments

A bubble bursts, then floats away,
It's filled with giggles for the day.
Chase not the clock, just seize the fun,
For laughter rivals the morning sun.

Grab each moment, don't let it slide,
It's not found in books or in pride.
A tickle tick, a silly game,
The essence hides in a lost name.

Lost Pages of the Timeless Book

In dusty shelves, the pages hide,
But wisdom laughs, it's implied.
A chapter missed in every rush,
Is written in the quiet hush.

With every turn, the plot twist grows,
A slapstick fall, a friend's bright nose.
Forget the script, let life unfold,
For laughter's worth its weight in gold.

Gems Hidden in Dusty Shelves

In corners dark where treasures lie,
A sock or two, oh my, oh my!
Beneath the gloom, a tale unfolds,
Of birthday gifts, now bought and sold.

A mirror cracked reflects my frown,
"Where is the joy?" I turn around.
A lonely cup, a friend long lost,
Reminds me of my youthful cost.

The Paradox of True Riches

I searched the aisles for golden threads,
Not in the stores, but in my beds.
A crumpled note, a loaf half-eaten,
Riches of laughter, never beaten.

With every sneeze, the world bestowed,
A life of joy; it's never slowed.
Priceless moments, while I sleep,
Are worth the gold that I can't keep.

Whirlwinds of Unpurchased Experiences

A coupon book for dizzy dreams,
But none of them fit into streams.
I dash through doors that lead to grass,
And wonder how much time can pass.

With every step, the world spins fast,
Yet memories are my riches cast.
A flip-flop here, a laugh or two,
No tags required for what is true.

Voices in the Silent Canyons

In quiet caves where whispers play,
Echoes tell tales of yesterday.
I pause to listen, just a bit,
For laughter lingers where I sit.

The canyon's depth, the high notes soar,
While shadows dance, they laugh and roar.
These moments free, no price to pay,
Are treasures found in bright dismay.

The Collection of Intangible Moments

I searched for joy in every aisle,
But found instead a pair of smiles.
In boxes labeled 'hugs' and 'kisses',
I settled for a bit of blisses.

The discount bin held laughter bright,
I piled it high, oh what a sight!
I left my cart in sheer delight,
For sparkly moments in the night.

Signposts in the Wilderness

Lost out here, I see a sign,
That reads 'You're doing just fine!'
A squirrel nods with a knowing wink,
As I pause to gather thoughts to think.

The compass spins, I take a break,
Do I turn left or take a shake?
With breadcrumbs tossed, and thoughts in flight,
I laugh with trees until it's night.

Reflections in a Broken Mirror

In shards of glass, I see a face,
That laughs and dances in its place.
It shows my quirks with every crack,
An artful map of my track.

Each fragment holds a funny tale,
Of awkward moments, none too frail.
With laughter ringing through the hall,
I clear that mirror, stand up tall.

Fragments of a Life Unspoken

I gather bits of dreams misplaced,
In shoeboxes, all interlaced.
With mismatched socks and pens that leak,
I crumple notes, my thoughts unique.

A recipe for joy I find,
With extra giggles, love, and kind.
In every scrap, a story lives,
Of silly fumbles and what life gives.

Navigating the Invisible Compass

Lost in the aisles, I roam the spree,
Trying to find what's missing in me.
With a map that's just a doodle of dreams,
I wander through life with coffee and schemes.

Discounted laughter and sadness on sale,
But true joy? It evades like a snail.
I check the return policy on the fun,
It seems I've already hit 'zero' and run.

Treasures Beyond the Price Tag

Bargain bins filled with glitter and ties,
Yet the best treasures live in surprise.
The joy of a sunrise, the thrill of a hug,
Cannot be found in a store's cluttered mug.

I searched for wisdom beside the cereal,
Where prices drop when you wear a cheerio.
They slap on a tag for each grand reveal,
But the laughter we share? That's the true deal.

Echoes of the Unpurchased Soul

Window shopping for happiness, I stroll,
In a sea of fake smiles, I lose my control.
I pick up a trinket that claims to be wise,
But it just echoes back my half-hearted sighs.

The heart's not for sale—clearly it's absurd,
Yet here I stand, lost in words unheard.
I try on some joy like it's a new hat,
But it slips off my head; oh, imagine that!

Chasing Shadows in the Marketplace

I chase after shadows like they're on sale,
With a shopping cart full of whimsical tales.
Each corner I turn brings a laugh or a frown,
As I search for the sparkle that's not weighed down.

The clerk gives me tips on how to be free,
But I can't seem to find a good warranty.
So I giggle and trip, through this humorous plight,
As I shop for the mysteries of day and of night.

Songs of the Unsung Journey

In a world of shiny things,
I search for truths that sing,
But all I find are socks alone,
And a cat that won't leave me alone.

I wander down the aisles of dreams,
Past sparkling gadgets and silly memes,
The price tags dance, they laugh and sway,
But what is worth? Who knows, I say!

With every step, my wallet groans,
As I seek wisdom in rubber bones,
The laughter echoes, takes a flight,
As I ponder what's wrong and right.

In the end, it's just a smile,
Juice boxes and a funny style,
The treasures found on paths so wry,
Are worth more than a gold-brick pie.

Paths Woven in Shadows

I stroll along a twisted route,
With flip-flops that just don't suit,
I meet a sage, he's lost his head,
But offers wisdom on a bed.

He says, "Don't buy what you can't eat!"
As a pigeon lands on my feet,
It craves the crumbs of other plight,
Finding joy in a bread-crumb fight.

Through tangled trees and seams of fog,
I chase a dream, but it's just a dog,
He's barking thoughts, that make me grin,
Maybe life's a race we're bound to win.

Each wrinkle tells a story grand,
Of pizza nights and greasy bands,
So I'll take this path, through laughs and dance,
Chasing shadows, given the chance.

What Cannot Be Sold

I wandered into a thrift store's heart,
Where jars of marbles play their part,
A sign that reads "Buy happiness here!"
But all I found was a giggle and cheer.

The cashier laughs, she's missing a shoe,
Says "Price tags can't give you a clue!"
While I ponder the cost of my glee,
A rubber chicken makes a mockery of me.

We barter stories of days gone wrong,
For wisdom bought in silly song,
The laughter lifts, it cannot be tamed,
What cannot be sold, can't be framed.

So here's to the deals we never regret,
For happiness found can't be met,
In pop-up shops or online estates,
But in hugs and smiles that life creates.

Mountains of Intangible Joy

I climbed a hill of used old shoes,
With every step, I'm bound to lose,
They squeak and squawk, a delightful sound,
As I tumble into joy that's round.

The view from here is mixed with fun,
Socks on my hands, I race a bun,
Each giggle bounces through the air,
And even the clouds just stop and stare.

I met a bear who wore a hat,
He offered cookies, imagine that!
He said, "No cash, just share a joke,"
And with that laugh, the mountains woke.

In carefree scenes, joy fills the void,
In laughter's arms, we've all enjoyed,
For what we crave cannot be bought,
On these heights, true happiness is sought.

Beneath the Surface of Desire

I searched for happiness on sale,
In aisle three, near the ice cream trail.
But found a sign that said 'out of stock,'
Just my luck, I clocked the clock.

I tried to bargain, haggling hard,
With my wallet, an old joke card.
The cashier chuckled, said with a grin,
"True joy's not found, it comes from within!"

The Chronicles of Unbought Wisdom

I walked through life's great clearance rack,
Sampling wisdom, no skills to lack.
Yet found the price was quite a fuss,
The tag read 'free,' but cost my trust.

Each choice a riddle, a puzzle to crack,
I picked a guide with a colorful pack.
It said, 'Just laugh,' in big bold print,
But the jokes it told made my heart squint.

Seeds of Purpose in Untamed Fields

I planted dreams in a garden plot,
Watered them daily, gave it all I got.
But weeds of worry sprouted up fast,
Laughed at my hopes, like they knew they'd last.

I asked a squirrel for some advice,
He chuckled, said, "Just roll the dice."
With laughter's soil, I swore to sow,
And watched where silly passions would grow.

The Dance of Elusive Fulfillment

I joined a dance class, full of glee,
To twirl with purpose, to set my soul free.
The instructor winked, asked how I felt,
I tripped and fell, was it wisdom I dealt?

Chasing my tail in a waltz of despair,
Hoping fulfillment would somehow be fair.
But laughed my way through each step I improvised,
Finding joy in the stumble, oh how I prized!

The Hidden Currency of Joy

In a world where happiness is for sale,
We laugh at the price, it's a comical tale.
Finding joy in the weirdest of places,
Like dancing with ducks or making strange faces.

A dollar buys chocolate but joy comes for free,
Caught holding the sunshine, don't you agree?
We trade silly puns like they're precious gold,
In a market of giggles, our hearts are consoled.

Buy a new couch or unbox a new game,
But joy is a laugh that just won't be tamed.
Sprinkle some laughter, let worries all flow,
In the land of the goofy, that's where we glow.

So stash all your worries in a trust fund of fun,
Forget labeled prices, let's run and just run.
In this currency hoard, we'll count every cheer,
For joy is the treasure that we hold dear.

Recipes for Authenticity

Grab your apron, let's bake a new dream,
With sprinkles of honesty, let's burst at the seam.
Churn laughter in bowls, mix wisdom with glee,
The secret ingredient? Just be silly and free.

A pinch of weirdness, a dash of delight,
Toss doubts in the oven, bake them up right.
You'll find in the mixing, a flavor so true,
Authentic as grandma's old recipes too.

I'll trade your straight face for a quirky smile,
And throw in some charm, just to spice it a while.
Serve up your story with a dollop of fun,
In this feast of realness, we all get undone.

So let's dine on laughter, oh what a fine dish,
Where authenticity's served on a playful wish.
Forget the recipe books, grab what you can,
For the best dish in life is the joy of the plan.

Beyond the Checkout Line

The cashier asks for my heart, what a scheme,
But I can't pay that price, that's not in the dream.
I'll barter a smile for the bliss that I seek,
In the aisle of pure laughter, I'll dare to be cheek.

I'll take 12 ounces of sunshine, please,
And exchange all my stress for a playful breeze.
With each little giggle, I'll fill up my cart,
It's a treasure trove fluttering straight from the heart.

Got coupons for kindness and discounts for cheer,
In this shop of existence, there's no room for fear.
So skip the dull checkout, let's dance through the store,
With our hands full of dreams, who could ask for more?

We'll toss labels aside, for joy's our best find,
In this market of nonsense, let's leave doubts behind.
So gather your laughter, that's the ultimate score,
For happiness sold here is forever in store.

Canvas of Dreams Untouched

With brushes of whimsy, let's paint a new scene,
A canvas of nonsense, all shades in between.
Swirls of odd colors, quirks in the mix,
A masterpiece built with our own silly tricks.

We'll splash on some giggles, and strokes of delight,
In the gallery of jest, everything feels right.
Each doodle of joy, every sketch of surprise,
A portrait of laughter that dances and flies.

The critics may scoff, but they just won't get,
That a dash of absurdity's the best little bet.
So hang up your dreams where the wild things abide,
In the humor-filled frames where our spirit's our guide.

So let's toss out perfection, embrace the bizarre,
In the art of the silly, we'll shine like a star.
On this canvas of nonsense, our hearts will be free,
In the laughter we bask, that's where we find glee.

Embarking on the Odyssey of Introspection

In search of wisdom, I roam the aisles,
With coupons in hand and sarcastic smiles.
The shelves are all empty, it's quite a joke,
No wisdom in jars, just dust, and a cloak.

I check every corner for insights galore,
But all that I find is an old rubber floor.
"Buy one, get one!" the sign does proclaim,
But wisdom, dear friend, is not a game.

I wander through thoughts, with snacks on the way,
Pretzels and peanuts, they brighten my day.
I ponder so deeply, my stomach will grumble,
How funny this quest, I'll just laugh and tumble.

So off I will go, with my list and my pen,
For wisdom won't come, so I'll do it again.
A seeker of truth, in a world full of noise,
With laughter and snacks, I'll make my own joys.

Light That Dares to Illuminate

A bulb flickers on, and I'm filled with glee,
I'm bright like a candle, or maybe a flea.
The wisdom I seek is a lightbulb above,
Yet all that I find is a shadowy shove.

I search for the switch in the depths of my mind,
But all that I find is a bright, shiny rind.
The laughter is bright, illuminating the room,
While questions like midnight silently loom.

With each flicker on, is there truth in the glow?
Or is it just dinner—the pasta gone slow?
I slip on my socks, made of pure wool,
And dance in the dark like a fool on a stool.

So, here's to the light that we all try to find,
With giggles and grins, and a heart very kind.
For wisdom's a party, just lacking the snacks,
But laughing together can lighten our tracks.

Bloom Where No One Shops

In gardens of thought, I plant my seeds,
Watered with laughter, not consumer needs.
No fertilizer here, just mindful cheer,
As petals of wisdom begin to appear.

The flowers I grow, well, they're quite absurd,
With scents of old socks and chirping of birds.
Yet here in the blooms, I find silly hope,
With daisies in glasses, cheerfully dope.

I'm crafting a bouquet, just oops—who needs?
When blooms bring the giggles, I'm covered in weeds.
A dandelion crown, oh what a sight!
I wear it with pride, my crowning delight.

So join in my quest, through mud and through muck,
We'll dance with the weeds, not worry for luck.
For blooming is best where the shoppers don't tread,
With wit in our hearts and laughter to spread.

The Abyss of Yearning

I gaze into the void, with a sigh and a grin,
Where answers are hiding, yet laughter's my kin.
The abyss has a sale, oh what a surprise,
But all that it offers are puzzling lies.

My yearning is grand like a sale gone awry,
With dreams hanging high, like kites in the sky.
I dive into thought, then trip on a thought,
With jokes in the corners, wisdom I sought.

"Oh what is the meaning?" I ponder aloud,
As echoes of laughter drift soft in the crowd.
In darkness, I dance, with absurdity near,
Finding joy in the questions, no matter how clear.

So here's to the void, with a wink and a wave,
For in this great abyss, I'm no longer a slave.
With giggles and snickers, the woes get suppressed,
The beauty of searching is truly the best.

Time's Emporium of Illusions

In a shop where time does twist,
You can buy a smile, not a wish.
A clock that runs on laughter's cue,
But never tells when dreams come true.

Grab a jar of moments on the shelf,
Try to bargain with a playful elf.
The price is steep, but fun to seek,
They'll sell you joy in shiny chic.

A ticket for a ride on whim,
Where hopes can swim, but never brim.
A coupon for a carefree stroll,
In a maze of thoughts, we lose control.

So step inside this quirky place,
With treasures found in silly grace.
For every giggle that you spend,
You'll learn to laugh and never bend.

The Colors of Unspoken Truths

In a palette bright, truth hides away,
Blended with hues of a silly play.
You'll find some yellow, a splash of red,
But green's the color of things unsaid.

Painted stories on a canvas wide,
With giggles bubbling just inside.
A brushstroke here can twist the tale,
While purple whispers, 'Don't you fail!'

At the market of the quirky shades,
Pick a color that never fades.
But if you ask for that strong blue,
It'll smirk and say, 'How about goo?'

So mix and match what feels so right,
In the glow of laughter's silly light.
Dance in hues of muddled cheer,
For the truth is painted, year to year.

Reverberations of a Heartbeat

In a market where hearts loudly thrum,
You can buy laughter in a drum.
Some hearts thud with rhythm and grace,
While others just bounce in a silly race.

A sale on giggles, two for one,
With every beat, life's just begun.
The echoes dance in a funny tone,
Reminding us, we're never alone.

Each heartbeat comes with a unique sound,
A melody found in the joy around.
So tune in close to what beats wise,
And catch those laughs with wide-eyed surprise.

In this bazaar of sounds so sweet,
Every pulse brings a jig to your feet.
So laugh on cue, let your heart cheer,
For funny echoes are always near.

Beyond the Mall of Existence

Step right up to a grand facade,
Where existence sells all that's odd.
With aisles of wisdom and silly fun,
You'll fumble your way, but never run.

A cart full of dreams on display,
With clowns and jests leading the way.
You can buy a doubt or pick a cheer,
But in this mall, they disappear.

Try on a moment, a hat or two,
But each cost's covered in laughter's glue.
In the back, there's a potion for glee,
Just don't spill it; it's slippery, you see!

So wander through this comical maze,
Where joys are sold in quirky ways.
For beyond each door lies a surprise,
And chuckles linger like butterflies.

Values Beyond the Register

You can't buy joy with coins,
But try and see the price in groans.
A smile's worth more than a dime,
But it won't show up on the line.

Laughter's free, they say, you know,
Yet still, you pay the toll in flow.
No shelves to stock with dreams so bright,
They come alive in silly fights.

You won't find love in aisle six,
It's in the hugs and little tricks.
So grab your cart, embrace the fun,
The best things aren't for sale, bar none.

So next time you're at the store,
Remember what you're shopping for.
Values lie beyond the scan,
Not wrapped in plastic by some man.

Invisible Ink on the Scroll of Time

Time's a sneaky little sprite,
Writing stories out of sight.
Ink that glows beneath the sun,
Turns your woes to laughs, just fun.

We scribble dreams like kids in class,
Create new rules, then let them pass.
An eraser? No need to fret,
Each blunder's just a funny pet.

The clock ticks loud, but don't you fear,
Just dance around with snacks and cheer.
For every tick that sounds so grim,
A thousand laughs keep shining dim.

So grab your pen, let's take a dive,
In chaos we will surely thrive.
For though the time may seem so strict,
It's filled with giggles, that's the trick.

Quiet Revolutions of the Heart

In the stillness, thoughts collide,
Revolutions, but they hide.
A heart that beats a quirky tune,
Each bump and thump's a joyful boon.

It's not a protest, more a dance,
With twirls and swirls, they take a chance.
The quiet hum of silly dreams,
As laughter bursts at the seams.

Petty fights with pillows soar,
While real battles are nevermore.
Each fluttering thought, a chance to play,
Who says we can't be bright and gay?

So here's to whims that break apart,
The silent wars of every heart.
We twirl in circles, spin with glee,
And find our truths in parody.

The Song of Unfulfilled Longings

In the choir of dreams we sing,
A cacophony of everything.
Unfulfilled, yet we belt it loud,
In this crazy, mixed-up crowd.

Chasing echoes, a comical chase,
Wishing on stars, still losing face.
But the punchlines land with every try,
As punchdrunk hopes soar and fly.

The orders we place, never arrive,
Yet here we laugh, we must survive.
For every wish that goes askew,
An even funnier one comes through.

So join the band in this delight,
With longing hearts, we'll make it right.
For in the song's whimsical sway,
We find the joy in disarray.

The Canvas of the Unmade Life

In a shop for dreams, I tried to buy,
But the clerk just winked and said, "Oh, my!"
Paint and brushes, all on the shelf,
But not a single smile of self.

I searched for joy in a box of toys,
A rubber duck among the noise.
But laughter's free and often found,
In silly dances all around.

I found a jar labeled 'Best Intentions',
But there were signs of misadventures,
Like socks that vanish, a missing shoe,
Oh dear, the things that I thought I knew!

So here I stand, no price to pay,
For fun and folly lead the way.
An unmade life is quite a thrill,
No warranties, just laughs at will!

Ceremony of the Unseen

Under the arch of unbought dreams,
I juggle hopes, or so it seems.
Candles flicker, and the cake's a flop,
But oh, what joy in the coffee shop!

"Welcome, welcome!" to the unseen,
Where plans are wild and life's routine.
No banners fly for what's inside,
But laughter echoes, far and wide.

I raised a toast with glasses loud,
To awkward moments, oh, so proud!
A twist of fate, a dance gone wrong,
We sing our hearts in the silly throng.

So grab the joy, wear your best grin,
For the unseen's where the fun begins.
Step right up, no fee to earn,
In this strange world, all things will turn!

The Lighthouse of Lost Aspirations

In the light of dreams, I missed the cue,
The lighthouse shines, but I can't see through.
With maps in hand, I danced like a fool,
Chasing shadows, no clear rule.

As the tide rolls in, I lose my stance,
Expecting gold in a tiny chance.
But the treasure chest was full of socks,
Magic lost in the ticking clocks.

A beacon calls, "Come find your bliss!"
But what I found was boisterous bliss.
With fish who dance and crabs who sing,
What's more fun than the sea's zany fling?

So I'll sail away on waves of cheer,
Holding tightly to my doubts and fear.
In this lighthouse of dreams, let's toast the night,
For goals like jellybeans, they just don't bite!

Unveiling the Invaluable

I opened a box marked 'Super Rare',
Expecting gold, found only air.
Yet inside, a note with laughter lines,
Said, "Silly you, there's gold in whines!"

Amid the clutter of "must haves"
I found delight in the oddest jabs.
My hidden gems? A poorly drawn map,
Leading to joy—oh, what a trap!

In this workshop of the wacky kind,
I learned that joy is truly blind.
With socks for hats and spoons for shoes,
Why bother with regret or blues?

So let's unveil what cannot be bought,
In the twists and turns, our laughter is taught.
With quirks and giggles, we live the tales,
Where the invaluable is served in pails!

The Unwritten Book of Existence

In a bookstore, I did glance,
Found a title, missed my chance.
"Wisdom's Just a Sale Away!"
But the cashiers made me stay.

I tried to write my great big plan,
With crayons in my hand, I ran.
Yet each page was just a doodle,
And the wisdom felt like poodle.

I searched for answers near the pies,
But they just laughed, had no replies.
Even rhythms in my head,
Came out sounding like pure bread.

So here I stand, no book in hand,
Just the crumbs of my life's grand stand.
If wisdom's out there on a shelf,
I'll just keep looking for myself.

Threads of Purpose in the Tapestry

In a craft shop full of threads,
I asked if purpose makes new beds.
The clerk just laughed, said, "Try and sew!"
The fabric's just for curtains though.

I pulled a string, it pulled me round,
Got tangled up, had to rebound.
Each knot a dream, each color hide,
Why's purpose always on a ride?

The tapestry's a puzzle bold,
With missing pieces, truth be told.
My grand design's in a heap, alas,
Just like the last known piece of grass.

But as I craft this life of mine,
I find the beauty in the twine.
For every thread that leaves a trail,
Leads to laughter; that cannot fail.

Footprints in the Void

On a beach with endless sand,
I searched for footprints, made my stand.
All I found were jellyfish,
They looked at me like, 'What's your wish?'

"Where's the wisdom in your print?"
I asked the starfish, clear and glint.
"It's hidden deep, away from feet,
Try not to step on what's so sweet!"

I took a leap, a quirky bound,
Yet every leap brought me around.
With each small splash, I twirled in glee,
The void rang back with laughter's plea.

So here I sit on grains so fine,
No footprints left, but that's just fine.
For in the void, I dance and sway,
In search of meaning every day.

The Secret Garden of Unmarked Desires

In a garden where the wild things grow,
I sought a flower, but it's gone slow.
Unmarked desires, bloomed with flair,
Yet the bees just buzzed without a care.

I dug for wishes, planted dreams,
But daisies bloomed in radical themes.
Each thorn a giggle, laughter's test,
Who knew that chaos could feel like rest?

A gnome peeked out, gave me a quiz,
"Do you want happiness, or just a fizz?"
I shrugged and nodded, picked some weeds,
Turns out the weeds grow just like seeds.

So in this garden of messy cheer,
I found my joy, quite crystal clear.
With weeds and flowers intertwined,
The secret's there, if you unbind!

Treasures Buried Within

In a box beneath my bed,
I found dreams that I once fed.
A rubber duck and old receipts,
What a treasure, oh what feats!

Jars of smiles and frownful notes,
Half-eaten cake, forgotten coats.
A mystery of socks in pairs,
Where on earth have they gone, where?

A frozen pizza from last year,
Its existence brings me good cheer.
The hidden snacks of days gone by,
A wealth of crumbs, oh me, oh my!

Sifting through the cluttered past,
Life's true gems are found so fast.
Who needs gold when junk is best?
My heart's wealth is in this mess!

The Silent Search for Meaning

I searched for answers near the fridge,
Where leftovers hide and dreams do bridge.
The chili stew, it calls to me,
Is this my fate? A irony?

I leaf through books both thick and thin,
To find what's lost, my quest begins.
But coffee stains obscure the text,
Hints of joy? I'm perplexed!

I asked a cat, he just looked wise,
With judgment clear in his bright eyes.
He licked his paw, gave me a sigh,
Maybe meaning's just a lie?

In fortune cookies, clues reside,
But mostly, just a sweetened ride.
I'll take the winks and giggles small,
In search of truth, I'll have a ball!

Whispers of the Unseen Path

When I wander down the street,
I hear the pavement's quiet beat.
A squirrel grins, a pigeon scoffs,
Is this where wisdom really laughs?

The wind whispers secrets untold,
Of ice cream vans and stories bold.
I follow it, lost in a trance,
To find life's wonders in a dance.

A leaf floats by, wearing a crown,
It shows me life is upside down.
With giggles shared and puddles splashed,
I realize the meaning's not too brash.

In chasing shadows, I find light,
Through giggles, puns, and sheer delight.
So onward I go, come what may,
With laughter and joy leading the way!

Fragments of Forgotten Dreams

I found some dreams in a dusty drawer,
They were wearing shirts from '94.
A pirate hat and rubber shoes,
A bit absurd, but who can lose?

Each fragment shines a quirky past,
A paper plane that flew too fast.
The memories dance, a joyful spree,
Who knew my dreams hung out with me?

A crayon sketch of a monster tall,
With googly eyes, it starts to call.
It winks and asks how dreams can fit,
Within the chaos, every bit.

So here I'll sit, with colors bright,
Embracing dreams, igniting light.
For in these bits of fun and flair,
I find the truth is everywhere!

The Essence Beyond the Aisle

In the store, they sell the bliss,
But all I find is a bag of chips.
The secrets hide on shelves so high,
I check my pockets, just to try.

A coupon promises joy, you see,
But I can't trade my sanity.
I browse the aisles for witty fun,
Yet all I find is half a bun.

A self-help book shows me the way,
It's like a map, but leads astray.
I laugh out loud with my shopping cart,
For wisdom's cost is never smart.

The joys of life, not found in sales,
Are buried deep in whimsy tales.
I'll take my snacks and leave the store,
The essence lies in laughter's roar.

Uncharted Paths of the Heart

Maps of joy are hard to find,
With coffee spills that wreck my mind.
I tread on paths, both wild and flat,
And still I ponder, where's the cat?

They label roads and lines so neat,
Yet heartstrings tug beneath my feet.
With every turn, a chuckle bursts,
As I dodge life's bewildering bursts.

I stopped to ask a squirrel for dreams,
He gave me acorns, or so it seems.
I scribble notes on napkins blue,
For wisdom shared in nutty hues.

Each uncharted step a silly song,
In mismatched shoes, I can't go wrong.
What lies ahead? I'll take the chance,
With laughter leading my wild dance.

Whispers of Existence

In a world of whispers, I roam about,
Searching for laughs, with half a doubt.
The echoes giggle in a crowded street,
While I debate which shoe's more sweet.

Conversations with pigeons are all the craze,
They coo their secrets in feathery ways.
Life's riddles come with a side of cheese,
And a sprinkle of mustard, just to tease.

I ask the stars what's in a name,
They wink back at me, it's all a game.
Chasing shadows on a sunny day,
I find my happiness in the stray.

With whimsy crammed in my pocket's fold,
I dance through moments, both brave and bold.
For laughter's path is long, you see,
In quirky whispers, I'm truly free.

The Seekers of Solitude

They wander off with maps in hand,
To seek a truth in golden sand.
But solitude's a curious beast,
With snacks and DVDs, I'm pleased.

On mountaintops they search for peace,
While I recline, my worries cease.
With cozy blankets and shows galore,
I find my heart can't ask for more.

The path is clear: it leads to snacks,
With chocolate bars in cozy packs.
Who needs the world when I can feast,
And laugh alone, a funny beast?

I'll seek the quiet in the loud,
With giggles hidden in every crowd.
For solitude whispers the best of cheer,
And my laughter echoes far and near.

Starlit Pathways of Thought

Beneath the stars, we ponder still,
Searching for wisdom, what a thrill.
Ideas dance like fireflies bright,
Elusive truths that tease the night.

With tangled thoughts and silly dreams,
We chase the giggles, or so it seems.
Mapping joy where laughter flows,
Forget the rules, just strike a pose!

Philosophy's a wobbly ride,
A bumper car where thoughts collide.
We smile at questions, wiggle, and bounce,
In this mad quest, we'll never flounce.

So bring your quirks, and spin around,
In starlit pathways, laughs abound.
With cosmic zest, we seek and play,
No catalog for this wild ballet!

The Cost of True Connection

In crowded rooms, we wear a mask,
Yet wonder why it's hard to bask.
A joke's a bridge, a hearty laugh,
But ads won't show the true craft.

Swipe left for smiles, swipe right for cheer,
Yet screen-lit hearts can still feel sheer.
The price of fun is far too high,
When human warmth says, 'Just pass by.'

We seek the deals, the flashing lights,
But peace of mind is out of sights.
True connection's not on sale,
It's found in mischief, laugh and flail!

So toss the tags and checkout lines,
Join the campfire and share some pines.
In giggle-filled evenings, we'll rejoice,
In the currency of laughs, we find our voice!

Navigating the Depths of Spirit

In thought's deep ocean, we often dive,
Hoping to find what makes us thrive.
A rubber duck floats on the waves,
As we search for meaning, mischief braves.

We paddle through doubts, and sip on dreams,
While chocolate rivers burst at the seams.
With jellyfish wisdom and starfish cheer,
The meaning slips away, oh dear!

In whirlpools of thoughts, we giggle and sway,
With silly hats that spin our way.
The depths reveal, our quirks collide,
What joy to feel lost in the tide!

So grab your snorkel, toss off your fright,
In spirit's waters, we swim in delight.
No stores have stock for the fun we find,
Just the laughter that brightens the mind!

The Essence not on Display

In shopping malls, the glitz is grand,
But joy's essence won't be canned.
We browse the aisles for ready-to-go,
Yet genuine giggles refuse to show.

Unboxing moments, we spark delight,
While silly blunders make the night bright.
Wrapped in chaos, fun can't be shelved,
The spirit of joy must be self-excelled.

With hidden treasures in daily mess,
Bubbles of laughter, oh what a quest!
It's not on shelves; it's in our hearts,
In the silly dance of life's wild arts.

So let's treasure the glee that can't be sold,
In unexpected places, silly and bold.
For life's sweet essence is always near,
In the giggles shared, our spirits cheer!

Unwritten Chapters of Being

In a world of bright price tags,
Find wisdom stuck in parking bags.
Store shelves are filled with things to dream,
But none can buy a cosmic theme.

Once I found a sale on joy,
But it came with a sting of coy.
It whispered softly from afar,
'You can't just grab me in a jar.'

On aisle three, a grin caught my eye,
But the mirror reflected a sigh.
I realized the checkout line's bait,
Isn't the path to find your fate.

So I stroll past the clearance aisle,
With an absurdity that makes me smile.
For treasures dwell in silly places,
Not on tags, but in warm embraces.

The Light Between the Sales

In shops that dazzle and entice,
There's a catch you might think twice.
They promise happiness in a wrap,
But it's just a fancier trap.

The coupons shout, 'This deal's sublime!'
Yet time ticks on, faster than rhyme.
I bought a cozy sofa last year,
But where's the joy? Oh, let me clear.

Between the flash of every sign,
Lies the humor of the divine.
Just as I reach for what seems best,
I stumble on a toddler's jest.

So I laugh at the retail charade,
As I sip on my overpriced lemonade.
True sparkles aren't where you think,
But in laughter shared over a wink.

Unfolding the Invisible Script

They say the secret's in the fine print,
But all I find is a stubborn hint.
I scoured all the aisles, oh so sly,
To find a book on how to fly.

The self-help section looks quite grand,
Yet offers mostly, 'Do it by hand.'
I tossed the pamphlets, they made me sneeze,
Instead, I followed the wind with ease.

Each great journey starts with a laugh,
Not a list or a well-planned path.
Just roam where the odd ducks play,
And forget about the cashier's say.

So set your GPS to absurd,
Where nonsense blooms, and dreams are stirred.
For hidden scripts and maps run wild,
Awaiting a giggle from the child.

Pacifying the Inner Storm

When chaos strikes with noise and hum,
I shop for silence, but here comes a drum.
I tried meditation in the food court,
But the nachos were my last resort.

With each decision, I raise the stakes,
As if my heart was in free breaks.
'Can I get a zen with that?' I asked,
The barista laughed, my peace was masked.

To calm the tempest that swirls within,
I tried to bargain with a goofy grin.
But life laughed back with quirky twists,
Not on sale, just in the moments missed.

So I marched out with a grin so wide,
Knowing joy isn't sold—it's my guide.
The inner storm's just a dance, you see,
It whirls and twirls, and so must we.

Harvesting Stars from Dreamscapes

In fields of thought, I pluck the bright,
Glimmers of dreams in the moonlight.
With a basket made of cotton fluff,
I gather wishes, 'cause that's enough.

A star fell down, I made a wish,
Pulled it close, it turned to fish.
Swam in the sky with starry scales,
My dreams took form in quirky trails.

Each wobbly step, a wobble of joy,
Bouncing on clouds like a gleeful boy.
I twirl around with a comet's tail,
In a wardrobe full of whimsy and ale.

Now I bottle laughter, sprinkle it wide,
With sparkles and giggles, I take a ride.
Harvesting stars that tickle my nose,
In this funny game, I happily pose.

The Distant Echo of Being

In a teacup world, echoes dance,
Whispers of 'why' in a silly prance.
Who knew the void could sing so loud?
With sock puppets, we gather a crowd.

Chasing shadows with a broomstick grin,
Squirrels debate, is it a win?
The trees are giggling, at least I hope,
While flipping pancakes with a slippery slope.

From the attic of dreams, I hear the call,
A rubber chicken drops, makes everyone haul.
Each lost sock is a noteworthy find,
Echoes of laughter, intertwined.

So here I am, with absurdity,
Mapping my journey with ridiculous glee.
In the echoes, I find my beat,
Life's a jest, quite the treat!

Wanderlust of the Heart's Terrain

Packing my heart in a mismatched case,
Off to explore this whimsical space.
With maps drawn in crayon and a hint of cheer,
I tumble through portals, a pioneer.

Skipping over clouds on a pogo stick,
Tasting snowflakes, oh what a trick!
The ground calls out, 'You forgot your hat!'
It's a bizarre journey, and that is that.

At every crossroad, a sign that spins,
Tells me to ride with the kin of chins.
In this land where the flowers giggle,
I find solace in every wiggle.

So off I prance, with no clear path,
Chasing the rainbows, avoiding the math.
In this quest so funny, my heart just sways,
As I dance through the oddest of days!

Fables of the Unpurchased Journey

I wander through tales bought at the fair,
But the best ones? You can't find anywhere.
A fable thick as oatmeal could be,
With a twist of fate and a touch of glee.

A dragon in slippers on a unicycle,
Juggling three lemons, oh what a miracle!
The stories unfold in unusual ways,
Where time's disguised in whimsical plays.

I pen my saga with jellybean ink,
Each page a giggle, a wink, a blink.
In timeless absurdity, I find my muse,
In fables that sparkle with odd little clues.

So here's to the tales that aren't for sale,
In every adventure, I'm destined to flail.
From snickers to snorts, my heart takes flight,
In the comedy of journeys, everything's right!

Threads of the Unseen Tapestry

In a shoppe of wonders, I searched high and low,
For answers that sparkled like glittery-show.
But the shelves were all empty, just dust and a sigh,
No tag for the wisdom, just 'please do not buy.'

The fabric of life is a complex affair,
With patches of laughter and moments of care.
Yet here in the aisle, no guide or support,
Just mannequins grinning, a laugh we distort.

Moments That Can't Be Wrapped

I hunted for joy in a gift bag of dreams,
But found only crumpled-up old birthday creams.
The lady at checkout just shrugged with a grin,
"The best kinds of moments? They just can't be in!"

A box full of laughter, a ribbon of grace,
Yet none on the shelf—what a curious space.
With every unwrap, I just found more of me,
Stuck in the aisles of absurdity.

An Odyssey of the Unsold

In aisles of the absurd, I wandered alone,
Every item around me had clearly outgrown.
The jokes on the labels were dusty and stale,
As I searched for a punchline, but all I found—pale.

With carts piled high, I rode out on a whim,
Found socks with opinions, some too quirky and dim.
But if wisdom's a product with tags yet ignored,
I'll take it for free, though my wallet's outscored.

The Shadow of Forgotten Desires

In the back of the store of what once was in style,
Lurk shadows of yearning that make me just smile.
The dreams that lay dormant, like clothes in a heap,
Whispering softly, "It's fun if you leap!"

A longing for giggles, a chase for delight,
I tripped over hopes that were dusting the night.
So I laughed with the shadows, they laughed back at me,
For no price could hold what's as wild and free.

Sprouts from the Soil of Uncertainty

In the garden of thoughts, we sow our dreams,
But weeds of confusion burst at the seams.
Laughter is sunlight, we take it in stride,
As we water our hopes, with a splash and a glide.

Turning the soil, we dig for a clue,
In pots of our worries, we keep growing too.
A tomato said, 'I'm ripe for a joke!'
While carrots whisper, 'Let's poke fun at the oak!'

The flowers are dancing, a quirky ballet,
Silly squirrels join in, to steal the bouquet.
With rainclouds of doubt, they jump and they prance,
In this patch of absurd, we make room for chance.

So harvest the giggles, the silliness cheers,
In the garden of life, we mix laughs with our tears.
The roots may be tangled, but the fruits are all bright,
In soil of uncertainty, we cherish the light.

The Archive of Abandoned Intentions

An empty shelf holds plans that never took flight,
Each book tells a story, a half-hearted write.
Intentions like socks, they vanished as pairs,
In the chaos of choices, we laugh at the stares.

Dust bunnies gather, conspirators in crime,
Of resolutions made, lost track of in time.
A diary once penned, now just a dust mote,
Where dreams raced away, like a runaway goat.

The, 'I'll start on Monday,' becomes Tuesday's regret,
While the couch keeps inviting, a warm, cozy pet.
What was it I missed? Oh, something profound,
But it slipped through my fingers, like ice cream on ground.

Yet laughter remains, as we sift through the past,
The mishaps of years, they fly by so fast.
So let's raise a toast, to intentions gone wild,
And dance with abandon, our whimsical child.

Fruits of the Unharvested Orchard

In a grove where dreams do grow,
Pears ponder if they're ripe to show.
Apples argue, 'I'm the best!'
Yet plums just nap and take a rest.

The sun chuckles, 'What's the fuss?'
While worms debate on who to trust.
All the fruit with hopes so high,
But no one wants to say goodbye.

They mock the nectar's bitter taste,
'We're not just fodder for the waste!'
Lemons laugh at their sour plight,
Claiming zest in the moonlight.

So here in this wild, tangled mess,
The orchard thrives on its own jest.
Where dreams hang low, starting to fade,
In the unharvested serenade.

Glimmers of Hope in Hollow Places

In the attic of forgotten dreams,
Hope hides out, or so it seems.
Old shoes twirl in quirky dances,
While shadows play their sly romances.

Bottles clink like laughter's cheer,
Dust bunnies gossip without fear.
Cracked mirrors make faces blend,
Reflecting stories that won't end.

Amidst the junk, a spark awake,
Winking at choices we might make.
In corners dim and spaces tight,
Glimmers twinkle, just out of sight.

So, lift the veil, embrace the strange,
In hollow places, we'll rearrange.
For in the dark, our dreams ignite,
A funny game in the fading light.

Journeys Without Roadmaps

I set out on a trip one night,
No maps to guide, just pure delight.
With coffee cups and snack-filled bags,
I waved goodbye to endless drags.

My GPS? A squirrel's own plan,
Just zig-zagging like a silly fan.
With roads that twist like curly fries,
Adventures wait, a big surprise.

I meet a turtle, claims he's fast,
And in a race, I'm sure I'll blast!
Yet here we sit, a game of chess,
Trading tips on life's quirky mess.

Oh routes unknown, like candy stores,
Where laughter echoes and joy soars.
In journeys wild and unconfined,
We'll find the laugh tracks left behind.

Message in the Bottle of Being

A bottle floats on an ocean wide,
With scribbles inside from a playful tide.
'Help!' it moans, 'I'm all alone!'
'Can someone rescue this silly tone?'

Inside the cap, a joke unfolds,
About a crab who borrowed gold.
They say he's rich but likes to play,
In sandcastles that wash away.

It drifts past shores of forgotten bliss,
With wishes wrapped in salty mist.
Messages scribbled on napkins tight,
Wanna-be poems, oh what a sight!

So when you find this playful spree,
Remember, love's best in company.
For even bottles need a friend,
In the ocean's waves, on dreams depend.

A Journey Without Labels

In the aisle of self-help, I'm lost,
Searching for wisdom, but what's the cost?
The price tag says joy, but it's out of stock,
I'll grab a chocolate bar and take a walk.

The shelf is so full, yet empty inside,
They sell you the dream like it's a fun ride.
No returns on choices, just laughter and tears,
I'll take it all back, but for now let's cheers!

I wanted a map, found only a guide,
With riddles and puzzles that twist and slide.
The compass malfunctioned, it just spins 'round,
I'll dance to the music, I'll make my own sound.

Who needs a label when you're your own brand?
I'll pack up my quirks and my dreams on demand.
So here's to the journey, with knots in my shoelace,
Just count all the laughs, oh, I'm winning this race!

Treasure Maps of the Soul

They say there's a treasure, just follow the gold,
But my map's just crayons, and a story retold.
Directions all fuzzy, X marks the wrong spot,
But I'll dig with a spoon, give it all that I've got.

The chest of my heart is all battered and worn,
Sparkly trinkets lay scattered, transformed.
I'm trading my pearls for a lifetime of laughs,
And searching for treasures in old, silly crafts.

The quest for fulfillment, oh what a delight!
I tripped on my dreams in the middle of night.
Navigating giggles through valleys of fear,
The laugh lines I've earned bring the treasure so near.

So here's to the treasure that no one can sell,
It's buried in moments, where happiness dwells.
With maps made in crayon, let's all take a chance,
For the quest is the joy of this crazy life dance!

The Unpurchasable Truth

I searched for the truth in a clearance rack,
Found nothing but socks, a blue and a black.
The signs pointed 'yes,' but said 'not for sale,'
Guess I'm stuck with my whims, and delicious detail.

The truth's an oddball, it's wild and it's free,
It sneaks up on picnic, it hides in a tree.
I tried to negotiate with a clickbait ad,
But all that I got was a headache and sad.

They promise enlightenment in trendy stores,
But I found it instead on my neighbor's lawn chores.
Laughing like children, losing time is the key,
The truth costs a smile, that's the real fee!

So trade your desires for playful escape,
With laughter as currency, there's no need for tape.
The truth isn't on shelves, it's in giggles and glee,
And finding contentment is as simple as me!

Echoes of the Inner Self

In the depths of the heart, there's a voice that will sing,
Who needs a loudspeaker for such tiny things?
The echoes of whispers, they dance and they sway,
Chasing the laughter, they come out to play.

I tried to record it, but it wouldn't comply,
It wanted to tickle, not hear me cry.
So I threw out my scripts and went off the cuff,
Turns out my inner self loves to bluff!

It chuckles and giggles and runs amok,
Creating a ruckus, it's quite the shock!
I laughed with my shadows, and we twirled around,
In the echoes of joy, my happiness found.

So if you feel lost in the hustle and fuss,
Just listen for laughter, it's waiting for us.
Your self is a treasure, not meant for a show,
In echoes and giggles, let your true colors glow!

Ciphers Carved in the Dust of Time

In the attic of thought, dust settles wide,
Old toys whisper secrets, along for the ride.
Greg's rubber chicken? A quest so absurd,
Chasing lost laughter, the echoes unheard.

Philosophers argue with grapes in a bowl,
While socks go on strike, they're tired of the toll.
Riddles like pizza, sliced in strange ways,
What's the answer? We're lost in a haze.

A clock strikes the hour, it giggles with glee,
As time lines up sideways—what's normal, you see?
Pigeons in tuxedos, they're offering advice,
"Buy one hilarious moment, get two for your price!"

With giggles and wiggles, we dance through the breeze,
Constructing our thoughts like a life made of peas.
In the end, we'll find what was there all along,
A punchline awaited, in this silly old song.

Rays of Daring Authenticity

On the salad of truth, we toss in some cheer,
Dancing with vegetables, oh dear, oh dear!
Carrots attempt limbo beneath the big sun,
While radishes plot their own escape run.

Cereal boxes argue who's the most bright,
Frosted flakes winking, 'Your prize isn't right!'
In the chaos of breakfast, we search high and low,
For the spark of our essence with a side of dough.

Unicorns sell dreams wrapped in rainbow delight,
But it's the brown paper bag that makes life feel light.
Every moment a gamble, like tossing a die,
An ice cream truck drives by, making spirits fly.

So grab hold of the silly, the wacky, the fun,
In this crazy-old world, who says we can't run?
Chasing authenticity in masks made of fruit,
Let's laugh as we savor this life, oh so cute!

The Journey Beyond the Shelf

With every page turned, a trip starts to bloom,
Bookmarks are travelers, exploring the room.
Dust bunnies hide secrets like the best-selling tome,
While teapots brew tales of a faraway dome.

Board games on weekends play grand roles in glee,
As we dodge those old rules, too boundlessly free.
Dare to flip tables, scream, 'This is the night!'
Adventures unfold in this cardboard delight.

A fort made of cushions? Oh, what a sight!
Pirates and astronauts, we're ready for flight!
With each laugh and stumble, we get lost in the fun,
In the crumbs of our stories, we've already won.

So gather your dreams, not lined on a shelf,
Let's rewrite our scripts and be true to ourselves.
Through this journey of humor and bits of pure gold,
The tales we create are what's better than sold.

Embers of a Life Unscripted

From ashes we rise, with marshmallows grand,
S'mores turn to poetry, crafted by hand.
Every crackling moment, a giggle, a cheer,
As we roast up our laughs, 'til the end of the year.

A juggler named Jeffrey drops his best ball,
He stumbles and grins, 'Oh, don't let me fall!'
Life's a circus, rides spin and they shake,
But let's ride the waves of the silly awake.

With pies in the sky and kites made of dreams,
We chase all the wonders, it's not what it seems.
Cheese puffs are wisdom, with chips by their side,
Let's munch on the truths that can't be denied.

So dance through the absurd and sing without care,
In this show of existence, let's play if we dare.
The embers may shimmer, the path always true,
In a world without scripts, we create something new.

Mirages of the Heart's Desire

In the market of wishes, some items do gleam,
But they vanish like smoke, like a hiccuped dream.
With a camouflaged heart, I wander the aisles,
Finding treasures that fade, yet still bring me smiles.

A plush unicorn here, a dancing cat there,
But my longing is deeper, it's beyond this fair.
The best things in life can't be put on display,
Like a joke told at midnight or a bright summer day.

So I grab a cart full of whimsical things,
But the true magic's lost in the depth that it brings.
As I exit the door, feeling lighter than air,
I realize what's missing: a little self-care!

Now I chuckle and wander, this treasure I hold,
Is not glitter or gold, but the laughter untold.
From the mirage of wish lists, I learned to partake,
In the joy of the journey, for my own heart's sake.

The Ripple of Untouched Realities

Wading through puddles of dreams that don't sell,
I slip on the surface, oh, it's slippery well!
They promise the world in a flashy bright ad,
But the truth is more twisted, and quite often sad.

I sought for a potion to change up my fate,
But found only flavors that mildly sedate.
With a grocery cart full of hopes in my grasp,
I trundled away with an existential gasp.

The cereal box whispered of journeys most grand,
While the milk said, "Just chill, let's go hand in hand."
As I savored the crunch of my morning delight,
I laughed at my quest for the ultimate light.

So I ponder the ripples of choices I make,
And I toast my poor heart with a slice of fruit cake.
For in these bizarre waves, I often do find,
That untouched realities aren't hard to unwind.

Perceptions Unforged by Commerce

In a world full of gadgets that twinkle and blink,
I sift through the specials and ponder the link.
With a cart overflowing with items to boast,
Yet my joy is misplaced, like some unwanted toast.

I bought me a pillow that promised to hug,
But it's flat as a pancake, just a glorified rug!
It whispered sweet nothings of cozy delight,
But laughed in my face as it vanished from sight.

Oh, the charm of the trinkets, they beckon and sway,
Yet the best gifts in life hardly ever weigh.
They're found in giggles, in mornings so bright,
In the love that we share when we stay up all night.

So I gather my thoughts, they can't be bought cheap,
With a frothy cup of joy, let the chaos run deep.
For perceptions, oh dear, they can twist and can turn,
But the heart knows the truth — it's the lessons we learn.

The Tale of Unharvested Love

In the fields of affection, the crop seems so ripe,
But I'm left with a shovel and no one to hype.
The flowers of yearning bloom wild in the sun,
While I dance with the weeds, just searching for fun.

The whispers of romance float high in the breeze,
Yet I stand by the fence, just dodging the bees.
With my basket of wishes, I gather the fruit,
But the nectar of love makes me feel like a hoot!

So I plant my good vibes in the ground with a cheer,
And sprinkle my laughter, my cool friend, so dear.
For the harvest is sweeter when shared with a grin,
In the tale of unharvested love, I begin!

As the seasons keep changing, I'll smile and I'll sway,
In the garden we're building, come join the ballet.
For the moments we share are the seeds that we sow,
In the tale of together, let's watch our hearts grow.

www.ingramcontent.com/pod-product-compliance
Lightning Source LLC
Chambersburg PA
CBHW051637160426
43209CB00004B/691